T0195928

SOPHISTICATION
HONORS

SYNCRONIC DESTINY

Randall Lee Dockstader

Order this book online at www.trafford.com
or email orders@trafford.com

Most Trafford titles are also available at major online book retailers.

Print information available on the last page.

ISBN: 978-1-4907-7189-2 (sc)
ISBN: 978-1-4907-7191-5 (hc)
ISBN: 978-1-4907-7190-8 (e)

Library of Congress Control Number: 2016904951

Trafford rev. 03/24/2016

 www.trafford.com
North America & international
toll-free: 1 888 232 4444 (USA & Canada)
fax: 812 355 4082

This is the original document text that edited into this
documentary book. 1968-2015

Story
Tagline:
AUM... STUDENT OF BHAKTIVEDANTA, AC BHAKTIVEDANTA SWAMI
PRABHUPADA...TREMENDOUS FAMILY...PARTNERS...VERY BLESSED BY SRILA
BHAKTISUNDARA GOVINDA MAHARAJA...SCS MATH... BENGAL...7 NATURAL CHILDREN...8
GRANDCHILDREN step father 4 children...4 grandchildren all true friends...more than
wife...have best friend...ETERNAL LOVE, yoga love Author Documentary book now with
publisher...TRAFFORD CO. ALOHA KE AKUA, GOD IS LOVE... AUM JAI SRI KRISHNA
ST

CHAITANYA...Vegetarian 41 years...DHARMA DHYAKSHA DAS II INITIATED...1ˢᵗ INITIATION 1974, AC BHAKTIVEDANTA SWAMI PRABHUPADA...First experience with SRILA PRABHUPADA JAN, 67...CALIFORNIA. 2ND INITATION...SHRILA BHAKTISUNDAR GOVINDA MAHARAJA SCS MATH INTERNATIONAL...1994... MANY THANKS TO THESE MENTORS...MANY BLESSINGS... SURVIVED 2 types of malaria...104*+ fever...Vietnam 1969...The holy name saves EVERYONE...Jai Sri KRISHNA CHAITANYA...Organic...No GMO PRASADAM(food)... GRANDFATHER JACOB HARRISON DOCKSTADER, 100% ONEIDA AMERICAN INDIAN.

Bragging rights:
MOTHERS(1921)...LUCILNLDE MARIE...HOSTESS CHRISTOPHERS RESTAURANT...DES MOINES IOWA... PREVIOUSLY...2 MOTHER...ESTHER BURKE DOCKSTADER, GOVERNOR SECRETARY IOWA 47 YEARS...HONORABLE... NOW 95 YEARS OLD...JAI SRI KRISHNA CHAITANYA...IRISH, BELGIN, DUTCH, GERMAN AND SWEDISH...FATHER WILBUR LANG DOCKSTADER, BORN(1920) IN WASHINGTON D.C. AND WAS 50% ONEIDA NATIVE AMERICAN INDIAN AND HIS FATHER WAS 100%...Jacob Harrison Dockstader...FATHER WAS HONORABLE UNITES STATES NAVY VETERAN 1942-1945.
Previous wife's...Friends...Excellent children...SHARI LISA COEN KALB...ROBIN JO GRAY. FLIPPERS FRIEND FROM PORPOISE TV SHOW...FLORENCIA REGINA MARIA HUGHES... RAMA PRIYA DID.RETIRED MODEL TEACHER...WWW. SCSMATHINTERNATIONAL.COM...HIS DIVINE GRACE ACHARYA MAHARAJ, CHIEF TEACHER...SRI CHAITANYA SARASWATI MATH, INTERNATIONAL INDIA.

Work

Occupation:

ARTIST AUTHOR VIETNAM VETERAN USMC 1/3/7 INDIA CO.
H&S CO.69, VIETNAM VETERANS OF
AMERICA 1978...NOW BHAKTIVEDANTA YOGA STUDENT...
DHARMAGOVINDA ENDOWMENT
TRUST PVT LTD USA LICENSE STATE OF HAWAII 1982
ONGOING...PREVIOUS BOND 2.3 MILLION.
MEDICAL PERSONAL POOLE...HAWAII...OTHER BOND 3 WITH
HARTFORD CO. 1967, 1968,
1976...LAST BOND 1987...

Skills:

ARTIST...PREVIOUSLY BONDED...MEDICAL SPECIALIST...Silver
art NAVAHO...SILVER SMITH
TEACHER...CABRILLO COLLEGE 1972-1973.

Employment: AUTHOR Documentation Retried
GLOBAL WORLD SECURITY
ELECTRONIC SECURITY ADMINISTRATION, 1976 - 1977
ELECTRICITY systems security

Other names:

YOGALOVE, WHITECLOUD ALPHA THUNDERSTAR, DHARMA
Dhyaksha Das II

Oneida Indian Chief Shenandoah with partner Executive Chief General George Washington and Polly Cooper, Oneida Nation.

"We have experienced your love, strong as the oak, and your fidelity, unchangeable as
truth.… While the sun and moon continue to give light to the world, we shall love and respect
you. As our trusty friends, we shall protect you; and shall at all times consider your welfare as
our own." –Pledge by the patriot delegates of the Continental Congress to the Oneida
Indians, December 3, 1977
"Accept my best thanks for your friendly Care and attention to the Interest of the United States… I have often told you that the conduct which you have held would always entitle you to our Love & Esteem, yet, I repeat it with pleasure and sooner should a fond mother forget her only Son than we shall forget you." –Philip Schuyler, Continental Army general and Indian commissioner, message to the Oneida Indian, May 11, 1778.

Dharma Dhyaksha

Randall Lee Dockstader, Radhika
Dockstader, and Florencia Hughes.
Photo by Radhika Dockstader.

JD Dockstader, Randall Dockstader, Radhika Dockstader,
and Chandi Dockstader. Photo by Radhika Dockstader.

Randall Dockstader and JD Dockstader,
photo by Radhika Dockstader.

Randall Dockstader, photo by Radhika
Dockstader.

Bhakti Yoga Dedication and Appreciation:

Srila Bhaktivinode Thakur.

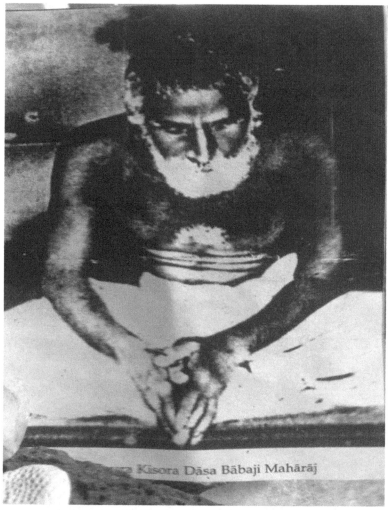

Srila Gaura Kisora Dasa Babaji Maharaj, Great
Grand Master of Srila A.C. Bhakti Vedanta Swami
Prabhupada.

Srila Bhaktisiddhanta Sarasvati Goswami Maharaj.

Srila Raksak Sridhar Dev-Goswami Maharaj.

His Divine Grace A.C. Bhaktivedanta Swami Prabhupada. He was my personal initiating Guru and teacher from 1967 onward.

Srila Bhaktisundar Govinda Maharaj.

Srila Bhakti Nirmal Acharya Maharaj.

Mahadeva Shiva.

DEPARTMENT OF VETERANS AFFAIRS
Board of Veterans' Appeals
Washington DC 20420

APR 1 6 2008

In Reply Refer To: 014DS200
C 25 523 582

Mr. Randall L. Dockstader
P.O. Box 762
Naalehu, HI 96772

Dear Mr. Dockstader:

This letter responds to your motion for reconsideration of the Board's decision of August 13, 2007. The motion was postmarked by the United States Postal Service on December 7, 2007, and received at the Board on December 17, 2007. I have been delegated authority to rule on the motion. *See* 38 C.F.R. § 20.102(b)(2007).

A decision of the Board is final unless the Chairman orders reconsideration, or the Board, on its own motion, corrects an obvious error in the record. 38 U.S.C.A. §§ 7103, 7104 (West 2002); 38 C.F.R. §§ 20.1000, 20.1001 (2007). The applicable statutory and regulatory provisions, as well as pertinent judicial precedent, provide that the Chairman of the Board or his delegate has the sole discretion to choose which decisions will be reconsidered. *See Mayer v. Brown*, 37 F.3d 618, 619-20 (Fed. Cir. 1994), 38 C.F.R. § 20.102(b) (2007).

Under 38 C.F.R. § 20.1000, the discretion of the Chairman or his delegate to grant reconsideration of an appellate decision is limited to the following grounds: (a) upon allegation of obvious error of fact or law; (b) upon discovery of new and material evidence in the form of relevant records or reports of the service department; or (c) upon allegation that an allowance of benefits by the Board has been materially influenced by false or fraudulent evidence submitted by or on behalf of the appellant. You have alleged, in essence, that the BVA decision contains an obvious error of fact or law under 38 C.F.R. § 20.1000(a).

The Chairman or his delegate will order reconsideration of an appellate decision upon the ground of "obvious error of fact or law" only when it is shown that it is probable that the Board committed an error in its decision which, if corrected, would change the outcome of the appeal. Obvious (or clear and unmistakable) error is a very specific and rare kind of error. It is the kind of error of fact or law that, when called to the attention of adjudicators, compels the conclusion, with which reasonable minds could not differ, that the result would have been manifestly different but for the error. Mere allegations that previous adjudicators improperly weighed and evaluated the evidence are inadequate to meet the standard of "obvious error," as are broad-brush allegations of "failure to follow

Page 2

Randall L. Dockstader
C 25 523 582

the regulations" or "failure to give due process," or any other general, non-specific claim of "error." The alleged error(s) of fact or law must be described with some specificity and persuasive reasons must be given as to why the result would have been manifestly different but for the alleged error. *See Fugo v. Brown*, 6 Vet. App. 40, 44 (1993). Moreover, reconsideration will not be granted on the basis of an allegation of factual error where there is a *plausible basis* in the record for the factual determinations in the BVA decision at issue. This includes situations in which a BVA decision reflects the reasonable judgment of one or more of its Veterans Law Judges regarding the credibility, probative value, and weight of the evidence.

Your motion for reconsideration, which has been carefully reviewed in light of the Board's decision in your appeal, does not demonstrate that the BVA decision contains obvious error. The BVA decision at issue contains findings of fact that have a plausible basis in the record; was consistent with the available evidence and applicable statutory and regulatory provisions; and contains clearly stated reasons and bases for the decision. While you request reconsideration of the Board's August 13, 2007, decision you do not set forth clearly and specifically the alleged obvious error, or errors, of fact or law in the decision. Your assertion of an ongoing claim in "70' 80' 90' 20's" is not sufficient. In the event you wish to refile your motion, you may do so by meeting these requirements. For these reasons, I must deny your motion for reconsideration.

Sincerely yours,

Steven L. Cohn
Deputy Vice Chairman

Enclosure: Your Appellate Rights Relating to Our Denial of Your Motion For Reconsideration

cc: VARO Honolulu, HI
cc: Litigation Support (01C2)

Department of Veterans Affairs

YOUR APPELLATE RIGHTS RELATING TO OUR DENIAL OF YOUR MOTION FOR RECONSIDERATION

The attached letter informs you that the Board of Veterans' Appeals (BVA or Board) has denied your motion for reconsideration of one or more of its decisions. If you are satisfied with the outcome, you do not need to do anything. However, if you are not satisfied with the outcome, you have the following options:

- Appeal the Board decision that you asked the Board to reconsider to the United States Court of Appeals for Veterans Claims (Court)
- Appeal the denial of your motion for reconsideration of that Board decision to the Court, but only under certain circumstances.

How long do I have to start my appeal of the Board decision to the Court? You have 120 days from the date the Board decision was mailed to you (as shown on the first page of the decision) to file a Notice of Appeal with the Court. However, if you filed your motion for reconsideration within this 120-day period, you now have an additional 120 days from the date of mailing of the enclosed letter denying that motion within which to file a Notice of Appeal with the Court. *Rosler v. Derwinski*, 1 Vet. App. 241 (1991). If you filed more than one motion for reconsideration of that same Board decision, you have an additional 120 days from the date of mailing of the enclosed letter *only if the Board received each of your motions within 120 days after it mailed its decision or its denial of the prior reconsideration motion. Murillo v. Brown*, 10 Vet. App. 108 (1997). It is your responsibility to make sure that your appeal to the Court is filed on time.

How do I appeal to the United States Court of Appeals for Veterans Claims? Send your Notice of Appeal to the Court at:

Clerk, U.S. Court of Appeals for Veterans Claims
625 Indiana Avenue, NW, Suite 900
Washington, DC 20004-2950

You can get information about the Notice of Appeal, the procedure for filing a Notice of Appeal, the filing fee (or a motion to waive the filing fee if payment would cause financial hardship), and other matters covered by the Court's rules directly from the Court. You can also get this information from the Court's web site on the Internet at www.vetapp.uscourts.gov, and you can download forms directly from that website. The Court's facsimile number is (202) 501-5848.

To ensure full protection of your right of appeal to the Court, you must file your Notice of Appeal **with the Court,** not with the Board, or any other VA office.

Under what circumstances may I appeal the denial of my motion for reconsideration to the Court? You may appeal the Board's denial of your motion for reconsideration to the Court only *if* you filed a timely appeal of the Board decision that you asked the Board to reconsider. *Engelke v. Gober*, 10 Vet. App. 396 (1997).

Remember, you must file your Notice of Appeal within 120 days of the date of mailing of the enclosed letter. Send your Notice of Appeal to the address above for the Court.

Can someone represent me in my appeal to the Court? Yes. If you want someone to represent you before the Court you can get information on how to do so by writing directly to the Court. Upon request, the Court will provide you a state-by-state listing of persons admitted to practice before the Court who are available to represent appellants. This information is also provided on the Court's website at www.vetapp.uscourts.gov.

VA FORM
JUN 2000 20G   **0220**

UNITED STATES COURT OF VETERANS APPEALS
625 Indiana Avenue, NW, Suite 900
Washington, DC 20004-2950

NOTICE OF RETURNED PAPERS

No. 98-2086

Date: November 17, 1998

RANDALL L. DOCKSTADER, Appellant,

v.

TOGO D. WEST, JR.,
ACTING SECRETARY OF VETERANS AFFAIRS, APPELLEE.

TO THE APPELLANT: The attached material, which you sent to the Court, is not accepted for filing. It is returned without action because:

Under the law, this Court must decide your case based on the record that is filed by counsel for the Secretary of Veterans Affairs under Rule 11, after you have had a chance to comment on it under Rule 10.

If any of it is new evidence (developed after the BVA decision), the Court cannot consider it. If that evidence is important to your claim, you may want to get advice about reopening your claim in the VA administrative system.

ROBERT F. COMEAU
Clerk of the Court

Attachments (to appellant only):

Various papers and audio tape, received with NOA 11/13/98

Copies to:

Randall L. Dockstader
P.O. Box 762
Naalehu, HI 96772

General Counsel (027)
Department of Veterans Affairs
810 Vermont Avenue, NW
Washington, DC 20420

Form 15
(Rev. 1/98)

Randall V. Dockstader

Favourable Points

Favourable Points give you the knowledge of your friendly combination. People with your radical, lucky or friendly numbers are your good friends or partners. Similarly people with your friendly ascendent are benefic and those with friendly sign are close to you. Again lucky days, years and periods of benefic planets bring prosperity, happiness and success.

Wearing favourable stones, metals & Colours bring forth mental and physical happiness. Lucky stone enhances the luck. Starting any important work at favourable time brings success. Meditation of the God (Ishta Deva) & recital of favourable mantra gives mental peace & eternal happiness. Dealing in or donating favourable items, cereals, liquids etc. brings prosperity at home. This way usage of favourable points in daily life can be highly useful.

Radical No	2
Lucky No	6
Friendly Numbers	2, 7, 8
Evil Numbers	4, 5, 6
Good Years	20, 29, 38, 47, 56
Favourable Days	Friday, Saturday, Wednesday
Favourable Planets	Venus, Saturn, Mercury
Friendly Signs	Capricorn, Aquarius
Friendly Ascendent	Aries, Virgo, Scorpio
Favourable Stone	Blue Sapphire
Other Stones	Amethyst, Blue Tourmaline
Lucky Stone	Emerald
God to Worship	Vishnu
Favourable Metal	Iron
Favourable Colour	Black
Favourable Direction	West
Favourable Time	Evening
Items to donate	Musk, Black Cow, Shoe
Cereals	Urad
Liquids	Oil

VEDIC RESOURCE
Astrological Services
www.VedicResource.com - 800 829 2579

Dear Appellant:

THIS IS THE DESIGNATION OF THE RECORD ("DOR"). It is a list of records from your VA claims file which were considered by the Board of Veterans' Appeals (BVA) when it decided your case. A copy of each record follows the list. Each item is separated by a sheet of paper that states, "End of Exhibit."

THIS IS AN OFFICIAL COPY which contains the documents that may be filed with the U.S. Court of Veterans Appeals for the Court to review in deciding your case. You must keep all the pages of the DOR, including the list, and exhibits, in the same order in which they were received. This DOR will be used by you or your representative during your appeal.

If you decide that additional records are relevant to your appeal, you may request that they be added to this DOR. If you are not represented by an attorney, the Court will send a "Notice to Counter-Designate Record" with instructions on how to add documents to your record or to accept it as is.

Thank you for your cooperation.

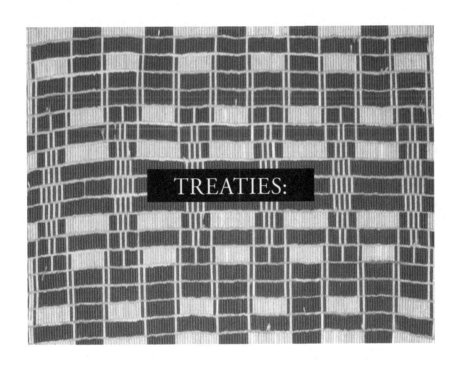

TREATIES:

Oneidas Brought wCorn to Washington's Starving Troops at Valley Forge
Story Created: Dec 19, 2008 at 11:14 AM EDT
Story Updated: May 24, 2011 at 2:33 PM EDT
Two hundred thirty-one years ago this month Colonial troops arrived at Valley Forge
During the American Revolutionary War, General George Washington moved his troops to
Valley Forge in Pennsylvania on Dec. 19, 1777. That winter was harsh and history reports
that about 2,500 soldiers died. As allies of the colonists during the war, the Oneida Indian
Nation carried their corn from their homelands several hundred miles to help alleviate the
hunger of Washington's starving troops during the winter of 1777-78. Oneida oral history
reports that an Oneida woman, Polly Cooper, stayed behind after the corn was delivered to
help the troops prepare the white corn which was different than the yellow corn the
colonists were familiar with. Prior to bringing the corn to Valley Forge, the Oneidas fought
at the Battles of Oriskany and Saratoga on the side of the colonists.

http://www.oneidaindiannation.com/pressroom/morenews/36439904.html

SRILA PRABHUPADA TRIBUTES by, Bhaktivedanta Book Trust International, Inc. www.sptributes.com Printed in England. Designed and layout by Jagannath Sharan das www.inajardesign.com

Dharmadhyaksa Dasa
All honor to maha-saktyavesa-avatar A.C. Bhaktivedanta Swami Prabhupada, maha-paramahamsa.

In 1944, Srila Prabhupada followed his gurudev's instruction to distribute "Back to Godhead" door to door, in chaotic political storm.

In 1967 Srila Prabhupada, beyond all heaven, to Ashbury came with maybe eleven... Srila Prabhupada came to California "to manifest Visnu's maha presence, 'a higher taste', the wisdom of eternal grace Song of God Bhagavad-gita, the infinite solace for the human race.

Promoters of the Grateful Dead, Jefferson Airplane etc, created s poster to come hear and chant... love's eternal call, one and
all.

By the 70's it was a much larger show, devotees and bands, Beatles and George, yes for sure, bhakti and siddhanta pure... IN 1974, 50,000 in Golden Gate Park experienced ecstasy from Srila Prabhupada...
In 1975, Srila Prabhupada created New Jagannatha Puri in Berkley, installing Deities for all.

Srila Prabhupada lives forever within his teachings...preaching, chanting, dancing and distributing prasadam is whole and perfect... love, forgiveness and mercy is the way, that A.C. Bhaktivedanta Swami came to say... peace and tranquility are yours forever in a certain way...

How and why Srila Prabhupada handed the holy name to all, is his eternal pastime... the Lord's mercy is free, and Srila
Prabhupada is the key...

Dharmadhyaksa Dasa

THE NECTAR OF INSTRUCTION by, HIS DIVINE GRACE A.C. Bhaktivedanta Swami Prabhupada
(Founder-Acarya of the International Society of Krishna Consciousness.
"ELEVEN LESSONS IN THE ANCIENT SCIENCE OF BHAKTI-YOGA.

Across five centuries and half the globe comes this compact guidebook of essential spiritual teachings. How to choose a guru, how to practice yoga, even where to live-you'll find it all in this invaluable work originally written in Sanskrit by Srila Rupa Gosvami, the greatest spiritual genius of medieval India.

Now translated and illuminated by Rupa Gosvami's modern successor, His Divine Grace A.C. Bhaktivedanta Swami Prabhupada, The Nectar of Instruction is the key to enlightenment for all seekers in the path of spiritual perfection."

Legal Criteria:

I Randall Lee Dockstader am the executive representative as esquire. I resolve any liability of, Trafford co., Random House Publishers; Author's Solution, of any and all legal liability. R.L.D.
I am responsible personally for all content of the publication, Sophistication Honors
Synchronic Destiny. The agreements are clear of fault.
Randall Lee Dockstader is executive chief, DHARMA GOVINDA ENDOWMENT TRUST. LTD.

Photo credit goes to Randall Dockstader, Radhika Dockstader.
Flower garden credits: Florencia Hughes, Jaganath Dockstader,
Chandi Dockstader, Radhika Dockstader.
All Oneida Nation photos credited to www.OneidaIndianNation.org and executive administration.
All Yoga pictures credit to Bhaktivedanta Book Trust executive chief office.

Radha Krishna, Supreme Personality of
Godhead.

Websites:

Oskanondonha, the lineage history:
http://en.m.wikipedia.org/wiki/Oskanondonha

Dockstaders in North American and Origin of the Surname DACHSTADTER:
http://www.genealogy.com/forum/surnames/topics/dockstader/58/

This book is dedicated to peace.

Printed in the United States
By Bookmasters